George Booth

Frontier folk

George Booth

Frontier folk

ISBN/EAN: 9783337148072

Printed in Europe, USA, Canada, Australia, Japan

Cover: Foto ©Andreas Hilbeck / pixelio.de

More available books at **www.hansebooks.com**

FRONTIER FOLK.

BY

GEORGE BOOTH.

REPRINTED FROM THE

INTERNATIONAL REVIEW FOR JULY, 1880.

NEW YORK:
A. S. BARNES AND COMPANY.

FRONTIER FOLK.

WHAT do we mean by the frontier? And what, by frontier folk? The terms came into vogue when tolerably well-defined lines marked the onset of civilization at the far West, and all beyond was wilderness. Yet to-day, with settlements scattered over all the Territories, the phrase loses none of its significance. It still has a geographical import, and another, deeper than the geographical, suggesting a peculiar civilization and a certain characteristic mode of life. It does not bring to mind those prosperous colonies whose lands, surveyed, secured by good legal titles, and freed from danger of savage inroads, have a permanent population busily engaged in founding homes. It takes us rather to the boundaries of the Indian reservations, along which scattered camps and settlements of white men are fringed; to lands which, though legally open for settlement, are constantly menaced by Indians; to those strange, shifting communities which sometimes, like Jonah's gourd, spring up in a night only to wither away in a day.

It is the purpose of this paper to present a sketch of the life and people of this frontier region as the writer has become familiar with them, depicting the types and manners of mankind, and leaving for more profound narrators the matters of statistical detail.

Social estimation and intercourse on the frontier are based upon a very short acquaintance. A large and catholic charity presumes every man to be that which he desires to appear. To pry into the secret history of his former life, to pass hostile criticisms on it even when known to be discreditable, is not considered a public-spirited act; for those turbulent energies or uncontrolled passions which drove him out of eastern communities may prove of great service to that new country to which he has come. The first element of success in a frontier settlement is that a sufficient number of nomads should be willing to sustain each other in the belief that "this spot is to be a city and a centre." The news that a considerable group is already gathered on any such foreordained and favored spot brings others; nor do the arrivals cease until a day comes when it is bruited abroad that some of the "first citizens" have revised their views of its glorious destiny, and have left it for a new Eden. The sojourner in such regions — he cannot be called an inhabitant — lives in expectation of the

coming settler who will pay him cash for his
"claim"; or else perhaps he devotes himself to
discovering a lode or a placer, which, if disposed
of, may put him in funds for a year's spree; or
again he may be a trapper, perpetually shifting his
place as the peltry grows scarce. These indicate
the respectable callings or expectancies of the solid
men in frontier life; but they are surrounded by a
larger throng of men, who hang about settlements
with the possible hope of an honest El Dorado, but
who in the meantime, and until this shall come,
take to the surreptitious borrowing of horses without leave, or to the industries of the faro-table, or
to the "road agency," by which phrase is signified
the unlawful collection of a highway toll amounting
usually to whatever of value the traveller may have
about him. There are no superfluous refinements
and gradations in frontier society. The citizen
is either "an elegant gentleman" or a liar and a
horse-thief. Yet even people of the latter description are rarely molested unless taken in the actual
practice of their profession, which they ply, to say
the truth, with such discrimination as to make in-
terference with them difficult; but if caught in the
very act and overpowered, their fate is sudden —
they are "got rid of."

In fact, homicide on the frontier, as compared
with horse-stealing, is a peccadillo. The horse has
a positive value; the thief, a negative one. Justice

does not pursue the man who slays his fellow in a quarrel; but if it grasps the stealer of a purse on the prairie or of a horse from the herd, his last day has come. Yet he always has the chance of escaping capture, and of playing in other frontier cities the *rôle* of "elegant gentleman" on his earnings, reimbursing himself in a professional way; and he may continue in this career even if suspected, provided he does not ply his vocation in those communities which he honors with his presence when not engaged in prosecuting his business. Personal violence is, however, mostly confined to instances where it is for the profit of the aggressor. The traditional free-fight, or killing a man at sight, is rare, probably much rarer than in the Southwest. Benton, the head of navigation on the Missouri, was the place where, according to the story, the early morning visitor at the bar-room, before it had been swept out, expressed his surprise, although he knew the soil to be good for vegetables, at the excellence of its fruit, judging from the large size of the grapes he saw on the floor, when he was informed, "Stranger, them's eyes!" — the results of the preceding evening's amusement. Yet in two visits to Benton the writer saw not the least sign of violence even in amusement, although he would be sorry to have some Bentonians around his camp at night if the horses were not well guarded, or to meet them on the prairie without sufficient protection.

If a settlement becomes permanent and prosperous, whether through commerce, mining, or agriculture, the first settlers sell out as soon as they can get cash in hand, and seek new domains. There are men who have passed their manhood in taking out claims, building ranches, and "realizing" for better or for worse, on a journey from Texas to Montana, sometimes taking in California by the way. Very often the wife, children, and stock of the pilgrim accompany him. Often a cabin is put up and inhabited by a family, with a retinue of cattle, horses, pigs, and poultry in the barn, only to be deserted the next year on the mere report of some better claim to be found further on. There never seems to be any real misery among these shiftless people. Their children grow up sturdy and ignorant, their stock and chickens multiply as they journey on. It may be a new stage-route which gives them a year's sustenance, such as it is, by their squatting on good enough grass-land to be able to fill a hay contract. Or they may go to a point near which some new military post is about to be built, where they can raise some vegetables to sell to the troops before the company gardens become productive. Or they may take out a claim on some really good spot, where permanent settlers speedily follow them. But as soon as they can see flour, bacon, and tobacco, and find a little in the pocket for whiskey and clothes, sufficient to

last for a year ahead, off they go again, — not so
much like gypsies, who will often revisit the same
spot, as like the Wandering Jew, pursued by an
avenging angel, driving them from contact with
steady and methodical people. Their household
stuff is packed in their "prairie schooners," as their
wagons are called, and on they move by easy stages,
seldom taking the trouble to pitch a tent at night,
the women sleeping in the wagons and the men on
the ground beneath them. There is plenty of grass
for the stock, and the weather is pleasant. There
is no especial hurry or worry : it is only necessary
to reach somewhere, in time to put up a log hut
and a shed for the stock, for the winter's shelter.
The little army of the United States, spread over a
country as large as the Roman Empire, does its
duty so well that there is only occasional danger
from Indians roaming away from their reservations,
and the military telegraphs are now so far extended
that timely warning is usually given if war parties
are out. So on they go, day after day, while at
night comes an encampment which perhaps may be
best described in these humorous words of Captain
Derby, in "Phœnixiana," during a criticism upon a
supposititious performance of an opera called "The
Plains " : —

The train now encamps. The unpacking of the kettles
and mess-pans, the unyoking of the oxen, the gathering about
of various camp-fires, the frizzling of the pork, are so clearly

expressed by the music that the most untutored savage could readily comprehend it. Indeed, so vivid and lifelike was the representation that a lady sitting near us involuntarily exclaimed aloud at a certain passage, " Thar, that pork's burning!" and it was truly interesting to watch the gratified expression of her face when, by a few notes of the guitar, the pan was removed from the fire, and the blazing pork extinguished. This is followed by the beautiful *aria*, " O marm, I want a pancake," followed by that touching recitative, "Shet up, or I will spank you!" To which succeeds a grand *crescendo* movement, representing the flight of the child with the pancake, the pursuit of the mother, and the final arrest and summary punishment of the former, represented by the rapid and successive strokes of the castanet. The turning-in for the night follows ; and the deep and stertorous breathing of the encampment is well given by the bassoon, while the sufferings and trials of an unhappy father with an unpleasant infant are touchingly set forth by the *cornet à piston*.

Nomadic habits, slight contact with anything human that is permanent, and freedom from the restraint which would be caused by the propinquity of neighbors, have fortified these people in self-conceit. Although they will in a few months desert all their acres for something more distant, yet the traveller who stops at their cabin and pays for bad food is required to "allow" that he has never seen a finer " claim " or tasted better victuals. In truth, never was good food so spoiled. The best venison of the country is sliced thin, put on cold grease in a frying-pan (they never think of first boiling the grease), and fried until it is as tough as a chip and as full of grease as an English-

man's crumpet. Once in Colorado a request to
have an egg boiled was encountered by the state-
ment that "the lady knew how to cook eggs — she
fried 'em." And fried they were, being put in cold
lard in proportions of three of lard to one of egg.
Another "lady," at the hint that a gridiron might
be used instead of the frying-pan for the venison,
seeing an army officer present, remarked, "If you
can't eat what we eat, you can go without. Don't
see the use of troops anyhow. We pay for you.
Understand Sitting Bull is going to Canada to fight
Fenians. He will find somebody to fight there —
never did here! As the woman was paid five times
the worth of her victuals, and as she, her "par"
and her "mar" could not have remained twelve
hours in their cabin had the military post near by
been withdrawn, her sarcasms were a little ill-con-
sidered. These much-isolated people look upon
themselves as Nature's aristocracy. Perhaps if
Robinson Crusoe were a king, they might be feudal
barons. Their social standing is sustained only by
lack of neighbors. But on their own dunghill they
have none to overcrow them.

The occasional traveller who may have been told
that there were ranches on his trail, and that he
need not take tents or camp equipage for cooking,
will, if he be new to these people, or have regard
for his digestion, find to his disgust that during his
stay he is a vassal at the castle of Giant Despair.

He is alluded to by his host as a "tender-foot," — a word which is supposed to sum up everything that is contemptible. He may have scaled Alps or marched with armies, but a "tender-foot" he will be in the estimation of his host, until he may be forced by circumstances to live a hundred miles further out than any one else, or unless he learns to carry food to his mouth with his knife. On the other hand, the only term of opprobrium which can be felt by these people is that of "Missourian." Why this should be so construed it is difficult to say; but the name seems to imply all that is worthless and disagreeable. Settlers from Virginia and from Georgia are sure on first acquaintance to inform you of their place of nativity with a pride which assumes that to have been born there furnishes them with blue blood; but the Missourian only mentions the last place he tarried at on his journey to "the setting sun" as the spot he hails from. Some of these good people, particularly those who left Missouri during the war, seem to forget that fifteen years have passed since that conflict ended. Their isolation has given them plenty of time and opportunity to brood over the wrongs of the South, with none to assuage their wrath; and they are still as bitter against "abolitionists" and "Lincoln's hirelings" as in the days when such things were.

The miners and prospectors are a much more

agreeable class. Their summer is passed amid
wild scenery and in a country abounding in game,
in pursuit of a fortune which may possibly be at-
tained by one among a hundred. These men find
a fascination in their way of life, and, though in the
main unsuccessful, continue it as long as health
and age permit. They pass their winter in some
town where they earn enough to purchase an outfit,
namely, gunpowder, coffee, flour, sugar, and bacon
sufficient for the summer's campaign, and a jack,
as the donkey is called, to carry the pack. Select-
ing a spot for their centre of operations, a small
shanty is soon built, and the summer passes with
much climbing, and much breaking of rock that
suggests wealth, while they keep a keen eye for
game and preserve a romantic belief in the speedy
finding of a fortune. Such men cordially welcome
the tourist, and gladly share whatever they have
with him, excepting blankets, which every man is
expected to carry for himself. They beguile his
evening by relating quaint experiences, and hint
solemnly of a spot where wealth beyond description
can be found. They usually work in couples, each
calling the other " pard "; and very faithful each
pard is to his fellow, becoming only more attached
in case of sickness or disaster. They are, as a rule,
an honest and manly race, leading a life which
brings out many good qualities, especially hospital-
ity, and, in injury or illness, even of a stranger, care,

kindness, and tenderness. There is no monotony in their career. Each day brings its incidents, greater or less, and is cheered by the belief that the *bonanza* is near at hand. Geographical distances are nothing to them. Fear they have none. It is a common sight to see a couple of " pards " on foot, driving the two jacks which carry all their worldly possessions, trudging through an Indian country, and informing you, perhaps, in answer to your inquiry, that they have come from the San Juan country in Southern Colorado, and are bound for the Bear Paw Mountains in Northern Montana, as they have heard that gold can be panned there. Many of them have paced the line of the Rocky Mountains as far as they lie within the limits of the United States.

In gold-washings, towns spring up as rapidly as Leadville has done, but the washings being simply on the surface and soon exhausted, the population migrates to other points. The once populous town of Georgia, in the Middle Park in Colorado, which was built by gold-washers, is still standing, with its Town Hall, two theatres, and streets of log-houses, and is now without a solitary inhabitant. Of course its Town Hall and theatres were of very simple wooden construction, but they were once really used for the purposes their names imply.

In a new town which is brevetted a " city " as

soon as there is more than one house, the rumseller
follows hard on the footsteps of the settler; then
comes the lawyer, who immediately runs as can-
didate for county offices, foments grievances, and
shows each man how he can get the better of his
neighbor.   If there be a military post near by, the
officers are good game for him, they being pecuni-
arily responsible, and obliged to obey the laws,
which seem to be so construed as to enable a sheriff
to arrest a whole column of troops even if setting
out on a campaign.   The lawyer's process of getting
money out of the military officers is easy and very
simple.   A practitioner secures a witness who will
depose to anything, perjury being looked on more
as a joke than as a crime, and so never punished.
The action or suit may be for pretty much anything ; it was, in one case, for the alleged illegal
detention of an animal which the learned judge
described as a "Rhone ox," further stating that
such detention was a "poenel" offence.   But the
unfortunate officer who obeys the summons, however ridiculous may be the cause of action, must
employ one of the horde of lawyers to defend him,
so that, whichever way the suit may be decided, he
at least is compelled to contribute something to the
support of the frontier *bar*.   In the Territories
justice is enforced when the United States judge
of the district comes on his circuit, but there is no
redress or compensation for the worry and expense

of litigation. If damages could be given against the concocter of the conspiracy, it would be difficult to find any property to satisfy the claim, and a hint of punishment would only cause him to remove to some other place. The army officer on the frontier has a soldier's dread of legal complications, and may be made thoroughly unhappy by suits which in the East would only be laughed at. A general idea of law is taught at West Point, but not more than one third of the commissions are held by graduates of the Military Academy, and these graduates find their general knowledge of law speedily growing rusty, while it never included the minute details of the kind of suits to which they are subjected by frontier pettifoggers. With fewer opportunities than the business man at the East of knowing the nature of court practice, they fall victims to any attorney who brazenly begins a prosecution founded on his own familiarity with legal tricks and the assumed wrongs of his client. Nothing, for example, is more common than for ranches to be damaged and hay or grain burned through the carelessness of emigrants, hunters, or other people who have camped near by, and on breaking camp have left the camp-fire to take care of itself: a wind springing up fans the embers into sparks, and these set fire to the dry grass. Now, although troops on the march are by strict orders compelled, on breaking camp, to extinguish their fires with water or by cov-

ering them with earth, the ranchman who can show
a burned fence or scorched barn (knowing that during the term of his natural life he might sue any-
body else but an army officer any number of times
without ever actually recovering damages) immediately finds out what military command has been
within some miles of his ranch during some days or
weeks before the fire, and straightway goes to a
lawyer and swears that the fire was set by the troops.
He brings eager witnesses to show that the fire trav-
elled just the requisite number of miles in the
requisite number of days, and that the barn or house,
if burnt up, was magnificent in all its appointments
and of palatial proportions. Suit is begun before
the nearest judge for real, imaginary, or conse-
quential damages against the officer in command of
the accused troops. This officer may know the
charge to be trumped up, but he is liable to be ar-
rested and to have his property attached ; and thus
he is subjected to such worry as will usually induce
him to submit to the most unjust drafts on his
slender purse. If the writer has dwelt at length
on this feature of frontier life, it is because the
abuse is keenly felt by army officers, and yet is
hardly suspected at the East.

It is a common mistake to suppose that an army
officer on the frontier leads an idle life. Rarely is
more than one of the three officers of a company
present with it, and this one must accordingly at-

tend every day to all the company duties. The other two officers may be detailed on special service, such as commissary or quartermaster's duties (and the latter in a new post will be no sinecure) or attendance on court-martial, or searching where lime can be found ; or they may be on the sick list, or guarding the wagon-train which brings supplies to the post, or absent on the leaves which are granted after continuous service. It is not infrequent for cavalry to be six or eight months on a campaign without seeing a permanent camp, much less a post where any of the comforts of civilization can be found. With small bodies of troops, where there are but few officers to form society for one another, the life becomes fearfully monotonous and dreary.

Old posts are deserted and new ones built so frequently that there is little danger of officers or men stagnating through idleness, even were Indian hostilities less abundant. An appropriation by Congress for a new post does not represent more than a third of the real expenditure. The other two thirds are supplied " in kind," that is to say, by soldiers' labor. The money appropriation is only expended for such things as the soldiers cannot produce themselves. They cut the timber, run saw-mills, dig drains, make bricks and mortar, carry hods, and plaster the inside of houses. The cavalryman is fortunate if he can leave off digging long enough to groom his own horse. Frequently one man is detailed to groom, feed, and take to water the horses of several of his comrades. The American soldier on the frontier is certainly a wonderful being. He is at most times a day-laborer, slouchy in his bearing and slovenly in his dress. His one good suit must be saved for guard-mounting, when his turn comes, or for inspection; and the nature of his unmilitary vocations uses up his uniforms faster than his clothing allowance can furnish them. He has little or no real drill, and has been known to go into action without previously having pulled the trigger of his rifle. He has not the mien or bearing of a soldier, — in military parlance, is not well set up. He performs the same manual labor for which the civilian who works beside him earns three times his wages. The writer has seen cavalry recruits, whose company was ordered to march, recalled from the woods, where they were employed at a saw-mill which supplied planks for some new buildings at the post, and where they had passed all their time since their arrival. On joining their command they were put on their horses for the first time, and started off, armed with carbines they had never fired, on a march of over eight hundred miles. If the recruit gives his horse a sore back, he will have to foot it; if he encounters Indians, he must fight as best he can.

Yet in spite of this treatment, — which is virtually a breach of contract by the Government, since the recruit is led to suppose on his enlistment that he is to be a soldier and not a hod-carrier, — in spite of his rarely being taught his profession, or shown how to become skilled in arms or horsemanship, the American soldier is subordinate, quick to obey, ready in expedients, uncomplaining, capable of sustaining great fatigue, brave and trustworthy in action. The previous lack of drill causes much difficulty for company officers when in battle, as the recruit must then be taught on the spur of the moment what ought to have been drilled into him in camp, where in fact his time has been spent in wielding a trowel. But history, even up to to-day, shows that the knight of the hod faces any odds of position or numbers at the command of his officer. If he dies firing a carbine in the use of which he is uninstructed (and even if he were skilled in it, it would still be a weapon inferior to that of his savage foe), he will be lucky if he has a pile of stones heaped up to mark his grave. If he lives through the fight, he will have become somewhat more accustomed to the use of his carbine, and in the next engagement will do better work with it. The country feeds him very well, clothes him tolerably well, — if he can do his duty so as to satisfy his officer, and if he does not catch inflammatory rheumatism from sleeping on the ground, he must be content.

Generally by the time a cavalry officer has reached middle age, his exposed life begins to tell upon him.   The cavalry, being mounted, are called upon to do most of the frontier scouting.   Some of the infantry are also mounted, especially the Fifth Infantry.   Infantry in such cases may simply be classed as cavalry, though armed with a better weapon, — the long Springfield rifle.   Marches in the middle of winter occur only too often.   In many instances the troops must march with cooked rations and abstain from lighting fires, lest the smoke may give warning to the Indians whom they are pursuing, — and this with the thermometer many degrees below zero.   As the Indian is as loath as a bear to leave his winter quarters, and little expects the approach of his foe, such expeditions are often successful, if a " blizzard " does not happen to blow.   This blizzard, as it is termed in Montana and Wyoming, or the norther, as it is known in New Mexico, Arizona, and Texas, is a strong, piercing wind from the North, which blows for some three days, and smites everything that is not under cover.   If the troops are spared this blizzard, they may strike their wily foe, who has evaded them all summer, and punish him, with no other casualties than those incurred from frozen feet and fingers, and in the fortune of battle.   The quartermaster's department furnishes excellent buffalo overcoats and fur caps, and men *can* march and *can* live on cold food in the middle of a bitter winter: but when the blizzard comes, the troops must seek the nearest shelter, and use every means to keep themselves alive. In many instances their wagons are broken up for fuel, as there are vast areas on the plains where no timber grows. In the sudden changes of station which the Government is forced to make with troops, by reason of the smallness of our army, much suffering is incurred, — as in case of regiments sent, without halt for acclimation, from Georgia or Louisiana to the British line. But after the troops have become acclimatized, and have learned to be always prepared for the coldest weather, they like the northwestern climate, which is certainly very invigorating.

On occasion of any military expedition, scouts are hired to discover the position and circumstances of the "hostiles," as Indians are called, for attacking whom orders have been issued. Their rewards are usually regulated by the importance of the information they bring and the risks they have run. Many of these men will do excellent service, and sometimes in a modest way. Many more, on the other hand, will lie *perdu* until their rations are consumed, and then come back with some startling but highly untrue information. They have proved themselves to be not too good to burn the grass, to efface the trail of the enormous body of Indians they pretended to have

seen. These men usually don a costume like that
of the hero of a dime novel. They wear long hair,
occasionally neatly bound up into a queue with a
snake-skin. Sometimes they cut out the roof of
their sombrero, to permit their flowing topknots to
wave forth like feathers. They use much of the
Indian's ornament, often adorning themselves by
sewing elk-teeth on their garments ; they also im-
itate some of the least excusable customs of the
savage. All of them endeavor to adopt some
prefix to their name. A Mr. Johnson, who was
drowned in the Yellowstone, acquired the *soubri-
quet* of Liver-eating Johnson, by eating and pre-
tending to prefer his portion of liver in an un-
cooked condition ; and he was as well satisfied
with this name and the notoriety it implied as are
Indians with their zoölogical titles.

"Squaw-man" is the name given to a white man
who has married one or more Indian wives, and
been regularly adopted by their tribe with whom
he lives. With the exception of being of occasional
use as an interpreter, he is an utterly worthless per-
son. He has completely left his own race and
taken to the ways of the savage, and is equally
despised by the whites and by his adopted breth-
ren. Many of the woodcutters who supply fuel to
steamboats on the upper Missouri marry, or rather
buy, Indian wives ; but they do not form part of
the tribal family, as does the "squaw-man." Often

it is policy for them to take wives from tribes which are dangerous to their safety. A wife insures protection from the depredations of her tribe ; and when her lord and master is tired of her, or wishes to form other business relations, he simply tells her and her progeny to go home. These men have the reputation of being most active agents in supplying ammunition to the Indians.

At the border of the British possessions, sometimes on our side and sometimes to the north, are several thousands of half-breeds who seem descended from French and Scotch fathers. They speak Cree and some of the other Indian tongues, but customarily use a French *patois* which is easily understood. Their government seems to be founded on the old patriarchal system. They are strict Catholics, and are duly married by a priest, who makes occasional visits to them, and insists upon legally uniting in wedlock such couples as he thinks have proved this ceremony to be necessary. They lead a nomadic life, trading between the whites and the Indians, supplying the latter with ammunition, subsisting mostly on game and buffalo. The latter they make up into pemmican, — a large bundle of finely chopped fat and lean, seasoned with wild herbs, and tightly wrapped up in buffalo-hide. This they sell, or keep for winter use. They travel in curious one-horse carts, in the manufacture of which little or no iron is used, the

pinning being done with wood, and the wheels
bound together with thongs of green buffalo-hide,
which shrink as they dry. As these carts will
float in water, an unfordable stream can be crossed
by swimming the horses attached to the shafts.
These people always camp with their carts in a
circle, the shafts towards the centre, and the carts
prove an effective barricade against any enemy
without cannon. Their stock is corralled every
night inside the circle. These half-breeds must be
classed more as Indians than as whites, as their
actions, habits, and beliefs are inherited more from
their mothers than from their fathers.

A great and always remunerative pursuit on the
frontier is that of cattle-raising. A well-selected
range, near streams which do not dry up in summer, and with timber, or such undulations of the
ground as would afford shelter for the beasts from
the worst winter's winds, together with a small
capital and reasonable care and exertion, will in a
few years produce a fortune, — and not only a fortune, but robust health for the herder. The season
when he is away from his cabin, herding up his
cattle, is mild enough to allow sleeping on the
ground. He is not compelled, like the soldier, at
times to endure the blizzard or to sleep in the
snow. Many young men engaged in cattle-raising
are of excellent education and social position, and
very much attached to the life they lead ; and well

they may be, as it gives them all the pleasure the frontier can afford with no more hardship than is good for them. Choosing congenial companions, they build a comfortable ranch, stock it well with books, and employ men to assist in the rougher duties, either by hiring them with fixed wages or giving them an interest in the herd. The day is passed in the saddle, the evening before a crackling wood-fire. The only time when great exertion is necessary is during the "roundings up"; then their whole property in cattle must be brought together, the young calves branded, and the brands of their parents retouched if effaced. There is no animal near by powerful enough to destroy cattle, and there is nothing to prevent their yearly increase. The Indians may kill one now and then for food, but cannot drive them off, as their movement is too slow. Cattle-stealing is not so easy as horse-stealing.

All these frontier folk eat, drink, and live, and after their manner enjoy life. We can perceive that they have occasional hardships, but they have pleasures which may not be so easily understood by people who live in comfortable houses, and drive in well-hung and well-cushioned carriages, or walk paved streets. A life in the open air, freedom from restraint, and a vigorous appetite, generally finding a hearty meal to satisfy it, make difficult a return to the humdrum of steady work and comparative

respectability.   They have their place in the drama
of our national life, for better or for worse, and
their pursuits and character must be recognized
and studied by any one who would comprehend our
great Western country.

www.ingramcontent.com/pod-product-compliance
Lightning Source LLC
Chambersburg PA
CBHW021459090426
42739CB00009B/1793